SORRY
I BARFED ON YUR BED

SORRY
I BARFED ON Y♥UR BED
(and Other Heartwarming Letters from Kitty)

JEREMY GREENBERG

Andrews McMeel
Publishing®

a division of Andrews McMeel Universal

Andrews McMeel Publishing
a division of Andrews McMeel Universal
1130 Walnut Street, Kansas City, Missouri 64106

www.andrewsmcmeel.com

17 18 19 20 21 WKT 17 16 15 14 13

ISBN: 978-1-4494-2704-7

Library of Congress Control Number: 2012948869

www.jeremygreenberg.com

ATTENTION: SCHOOLS AND BUSINESSES
Andrews McMeel books are available at quantity discounts with bulk purchase for educational, business, or sales promotional use. For information, please e-mail the Andrews McMeel Publishing Special Sales Department: specialsales@amuniversal.com.

For my wonderful mother-in-law, Arlene

My Lady,

Since domestic kitties shredded their first rolls of ancient Egyptian toilet papyrus, we have earned our keep by ridding homes of pests. We have banished mice from barns and feather dusters from tables. We have scoured windowsills for half-dead flies, terrorized untied shoelaces, and even made our force known to the tails of sleeping puppy dogs. And now, my human, allow me to protect you from the latest scourge: red laser dots.

We do not know where these red dots come from. Some suspect they live in a penlike object. That's why kitties knock all pens off countertops—to stop the red dot menace before it starts. And we know they make you nervous, because every time they appear and we swat them, you laugh.

But never fear; I will fight the red dot whenever it appears, even if it leads me right into a wall and I bump my head.

Love,
Hendrix

Name: Hendrix
Age: 3½ Years
Re: Stand back, my liege, the red dot attacks

Dear Two-legged Mommy with No Tail,

I know that it's wrong to purr for one parent more than another, but you could learn a few things from Furry Mommy. First of all, Furry Mommy never shoos me off her bed. But you hog your big bed all to yourself—and you don't even have your name embroidered on it. And when I do try to climb back onto your bed, rather than throw me off like you do, Furry Mommy climbs up with me if you're not looking. Furry Mommy also understands the importance of having dinner together as a family. Any time you refill my bowl, Furry Mommy runs right up and eats my cat food with me. But you eat alone at the kitchen table. When I try to jump up to join you, you say, "Get down, Tippy!" Furry Mommy lets me bite her ears, and she likes to play chase. All you like to do is take pictures of me wearing baby bonnets.

But you do make the food appear, and even as a kitty I understand that someone has to wear the pants in this family. The last time you tried to put pants on Furry Mommy, she whined and shook her legs 'til the pants fell off.

Love,
Tippy

Name: Tippy
Age: 5 Months
Re: Tippy has two mommies

Name: Dakota
Age: 8 Years
Re: Don't wake me! I'm dreaming of new places to sleep

Dear Insomniac,

I totally know what you mean when you say it's hard to get a good night's sleep (especially with me purring in your ear). I mean, the only places I can really get any rest are the wheel wells of cars, flowerpots, the neighbor's doghouse, the toaster oven if left open, most backpacks, underneath a lawn mower, a dry sink, a warm backyard fence, sock drawers, that bag you keep your wedding dress in, an evacuated underground bee's nest, an old suitcase, the branches of a Christmas tree, this banister, or any flat surface. It's torture.

Love,
Dakota

Dear Kitty Restaurant Owner,

Let me begin my review of your establishment by complimenting you on the cat-friendly atmosphere. Most restaurants pretentiously serve food on a table, and you can only get a taste when the human becomes distracted or gets up to use the potty. I've even been thrown off a table for checking the temperature of a dish with my tail! It's enough to make you feel like you weren't allowed to eat from the same plate. But the way you dumped the food right on the floor made me feel like I was the only one who would be eating it.

The service was also very nice. Normally, when food is served, they say, "Bon appétit." But when this food was dropped, you said, "Son of a bitch!"—even though I saw no puppies.

As for the cat food itself, while I did like the pile of worms, I couldn't tell if they were savory chicken, beef, liver, or seafood flavor. And I was disappointed that the green things were not lizards. But they were covered in a yummy sauce, so I was able to lick them at least.

All in all, I thought it was a nice dining experience. The only major recommendation is that the server should've also dropped a fortune cookie at the end of the meal, so that I'd have something to bat around.

Love,
Ili

Name: Ili
Age: 3½ Years
Re: I hope there's no MSG—it makes my tongue feel sandpapery

Name: Loli
Age: 10 Years
Re: I'm the only father he's ever known

Dear Adoption Lawyer,

Theodora and I have been together for as far back as I can remember, which, if cat memory serves me correctly, is about sixteen hours. Where did we meet? I know it's going to sound cliché, but we met online—by which I mean we were *lying on* the bed. When our eyes met, we just stared at each other—she was so taken by me that she never even blinked. Junior was also there, but he'd fallen over. I strolled up, sniffed her, and groomed her ear. She was speechless. Luckily, I happen to be into the soft, silent type.

Theodora's not that affectionate, but I know she loves me. And she is not possessive at all. She never asks me where I've been, or why I smell like goldfish. And Junior? I've never met a better-behaved kitten in all my life. That's why I'd like to adopt him. I know his mother wants him to have a stable male influence—and you can't get more stable than always landing on your feet.

Love,
Loli

Dear Potential Purchaser of Many Cotton Swabs,

We know it's adoption day, and you're here to take one of us home. That's why you keep staring. It's okay, we know you've never seen anything quite as beautiful as Sphynx kitties. Most people find us so stunning, they can't even believe we're cats. Believe it or not, some humans are jealous, and refuse to admit how cute we are. They call us meowing rats! But don't let the deep wrinkes on our foreheads fool you—we're not worried. We know we're special. And once people have us around their house for a while, they'll see that we're nothing to sneeze at. Mostly because we're hypoallergenic.

Love,
Blixa, Tiramisu, and Zabaglione

Name: Blixa, Tiramisu, and Zabaglione
Age: 3 Months
Re: Don't adopt us just because you miss your grandfather

Name: Bubba
Age: 8 Years
Re: Don't be so cold, baby

Dear My Beloved Crazy Cat Lady,

Normally, a kitty would never share his human. But I'm a little worried about you ever since you tried to take me as your plus one to your cousin's wedding. I think you might need some companionship that doesn't use a cat box. As you can see, I am a great kisser and a master seducer. Once I rub my gums on this cold piece of iron, I will have ruined it for all other cats. And lucky for you, I can also seduce humans. Let me give you some tips.

First, walk toward the human you want. Then stop for no reason. If you are in heat, howl. But don't howl like you do in the shower, or he'll think you're injured and want you to hide under the couch until you die. Next, keep walking toward him, until you're about a foot away. When he reaches for you, just flop down on your back. Let him scratch your belly for a second—just a taste!—then suddenly bite him. Finally, get up, and weave your way through his legs. Trust me, this drives humans mad. He might even fall head over heels for you right there.

Love,
Bubba

Dear Slave to Feline Fashion,

We kitties allow you to share our homes, occasionally open our hearts to you, and thoughtfully try to bury any food we don't like by scraping in vain at the wooden kitchen floor. And what's our thanks? Being humiliatingly shaved to resemble a lion! You wonder why kitties occasionally take up with zoo gorillas. That's because they respect fur. And no zoo gorilla ever thought we'd look cuter pretending to be one of our cat cousins. How would you like it if I asked you to wear your hair like your hotter younger sister? Sure, I'd tell you that I want you to cut your hair so you'll stay cooler in the summer, or keep your hair from matting. But you'd know the truth: I am just entertaining myself by shaving your butt.

Conditional love,
Muffin

Name: Muffin
Age: 1 Year
Re: I'd be lion if I said I liked it

Name: Mia

Age: 6 Years

Re: Can your cat come out and hiss?

Dear Door Opener,

Hey, I didn't expect to see you. Where's Boots? He usually comes to this window so we can hiss at each other. Can you ask him if he can come out and play—or at the very least look at me and arch his back? Pleeeease . . . I have no one to play with today. I promise we won't fight. You won't have to separate us. And after a while of howling, we'll even sit awkwardly near each other on your front steps. The arrogant birdies won't play with me. I think the jingle of my collar adds a nice backbeat to the sound of frantically screeching blackbirds. But they leave before I can even extend my paw in eating—er, I mean, greeting. And the other neighbor's dog is in the house, so I can't walk along the back fence to antagonize him.

Well, at least tell Boots I stopped by—or I can leave him my number in your garden.

Love,
Mia

Dear Soon-to-Be Floor Mopper,

I know you said it's "in the door, under tinfoil." But where? There are, like, three things covered in foil, and there are two shelves in the door. Care to be more specific? Just because my eyes glow at night doesn't mean I have X-ray vision. I know you think kitties are lower maintenance than doggies, but that doesn't mean you can be vague about where my can of food is. How would you like it if I were vague about where my litter box was? And speaking of litter boxes, maybe I'd be able to smell which one's the cat food if my box weren't a foot away from the fridge. All I can smell is that you seem to have lost your clump scooper. How can you put my potty in the kitchen, and then get angry when I drink from the toilet? I mean, it's not like you care about hygiene—you've got a cat in your refrigerator.

Love,
Charlie

Name: Charlie
Age: 16 Months
Re: I know you said "in the door," but where?

Name: Jillian
Age: 3 Months
Re: How much do you think I can stand?

Dear Distracted Human Male,

You know, most kitties only stand on two feet to watch a bird through a window, or sniff a treat. But I'm doing it because I have to compete with Little Miss Biped behind me. You may think I seem needy or attention starved for standing on two feet for a few seconds, but she is always standing on two feet. Do you really want someone who is too insecure to get down on all fours for you? Sure, I might follow you into the bathroom and try to sit on your lap while you poop. But that's just so you know I care. Do you think she'd do that? Do you think she'd sleep on your face the way I would? A woman like that won't be happy eating from a can every night. But I'll come running the minute you crack the seal. Plus, she has no whiskers. She'll bang into stuff at night and wake you up.

I think it's obvious who can make you happier. Please don't make me beg.

Love,
Jillian

Dear Stain Pretreater,

Thank you for running in here after hearing my prebarf howl, but I'm afraid you're too late. There will be no, "Quick, grab the kitty and put him in the yard!" this time. And although it is most unkitty-like to apologize for anything, I am sorry I barfed on your bed. I was sleeping on it, and now I have to get up. For that, I am truly sorry.

In the future, I will make more of an effort to barf in the appropriate place, such as on the bathroom rug. That way you'll have a nice present to step into barefoot in the middle of the night. I don't know why this barf snuck up on me so quickly. Maybe I caught a bug?

Love,
Isaac

Name: Isaac

Age: 7 Years

Re: Sorry I barfed on your bed (the bathroom rug is my preferred location)

Name: Maggie
Age: 2 Years
Re: The laundrocat: Where every coat is a fur coat

Dear Client,

Let's see, how many pieces do you have? Three shirts, a pair of sweats . . . good, and wow, a ton of socks! I can definitely shed on all of this. Come back after you've sat on the couch for an hour and warmed it up. I will take your place on the warm spot and your clothes in this basket will be ready for pickup. If you need anything starched, please let me know now so I can cough up a wet hairball. Whatever piece of clothes it dries on will be nice and stiff. Also, if you still feel there is not enough of my fur on the clothes once they've been folded, just leave them on the bed, and I will sleep on them again. I promise not to get off until they're so furry they look like a human cat costume, even if that means repeatedly jumping back onto your clean clothes every time you throw me off.

Love and that will be $3.95,
Maggie

Dear Provider of Turn-down Service,

No, I'm not getting out of bed. I have accommodated your weird habit of sleeping only at night for far too long. Every kitty knows you should sleep during the day, so at night you can scare children by pawing open cabinets and making them think the house is haunted. Nighttime is for spazzing out and knocking vases off of tables. The only time I hear you spaz out at night is when you have another human sleep over.

And what's with only getting eight hours of sleep? Don't you know the daily minimum is sixteen? No wonder your legs and armpits keep losing all their fur. Every time you start to grow a nice coat, the phone rings, and you say, "Yes, I'd love to go out." Then I follow you into the bathroom to watch you shower, and suddenly all your fur is gone! You should be in bed sleeping two-thirds of your life away like me. And who is rude enough to call at four o'clock in the afternoon—don't they know it's nap time?

Love,
Daisy

Name: Daisy

Age: 5 Years

Re: How do you expect me to get through the day on only twelve hours of sleep?

Name: Cherry
Age: 5 Weeks
Re: Worst spa treatment ever

Dear Clump Scooper,

At first I was excited. You picked me up, and scratched me on my head, and I was a happy Cherry kitty. Then you brought me into the kitchen, and I thought, "I must be getting a treat for being so adorable." And then the water started running. "I'm not thirsty," I meowed. But I guess you don't speak cat. So, I tried sign language, and flailed my paws in the kitty sign for, "Stop. That is a lot of water, and I am a little kitten." But you didn't get the message. I tried biting your hand and scratching, but it was too late. Not too late for me, that is . . . too late for you.

Sleep with your eyes open,
Cherry

Dear Party Pooper,

You wanna know why I eat grass? Because sometimes I just can't deal with life, okay! Some days my hairballs are just bringing me down, and all I want to do is cough them up. So, yeah, I have a little grass. It helps with the nausea—by which, I mean it makes me nauseous enough to finally throw up the blockage. You say the grass makes me antisocial, but hey, do you really want me sitting on your lap when I'm about to puke a spring roll? You should lighten up, dude. I know I feel much lighter after a good, grass-fed barf. Maybe you should try it sometime.

Look, I know you love me. You're just worried that grass is a gateway plant, and before I know it I'll be hanging out with strays and eating poinsettias. But if you tried grass, you'd see that it also helps with constipation and provides essential nutrients. Poinsettias are toxic to kitties; I'd never touch that stuff. But grass is medicinal, man. They should legalize it.

Love,
Macho

Name: Macho
Age: 15 Years
Re: Dude, it's medicinal

Name: Didjeradoo
Age: 16 Years
Re: Don't flatter yourself; it's involuntary

Dear Butt Scratcher,

Thousands of years ago, when kitties first domesticated humans, we did it so that someone would scratch our butts. We also trained you to scoop our clumps and hunt cans of tuna. But scratching our furry fannies is really why we allow you to share our homes. Before you start getting all full of yourself, you should know that my raised tail is not the offer it appears to be. "Elevator Butt" is actually a leftover response from when I was a kitty and my mommy would help me go potty. That's right, Butt Scratcher, you are my very own personal laxative! Though, now it just feels good, and it really doesn't help me go potty. But don't feel bad, Butt Scratcher. When I go potty, I do think of you—especially when it's in the living room while you're away on a business trip.

Love,
Didjeradoo

Dear Fellow Bird-Watcher,

I'm so happy you've decided to join me for some bird hunt—er, um, watching. I have a great ~~appetite~~ appreciation for birds. Do you see that beautiful red-headed thing? Well, according to the copy of *Bird Watcher's Digest* (the leading authority on which birdies you should digest), that is called a house finch! You might not recognize it with its head still attached. But that's what they look like before they've been decapitated, gift wrapped, and left on your doorstep. And that over there is a sparrow. You might know it from its common name, "mysterious pile of feathers on the back porch."

Hey, why do you have a jingly collar in your hand? Can't you see I'm trying to get close to nature?

Love but with annoyed tail flickers,
Fuzzy Wuzzy

Name: Fuzzy Wuzzy
Age: 2 Years
Re: Welcome to the kitty ornithological society

Name: Coco
Age: 14 Years
Re: It's a black cat thing; you wouldn't understand

Dear Bewitched Bed Warmer,

Why is it that every time your mom visits, you vacuum up my shed fur and then lock me in the bathroom? Are you embarrassed to be with me? You know, one day she's just going to have to accept that you're with a black cat. It's the twenty-first century, and she still thinks I'm a witch. If I'm a witch, then why do I run from the broom? Whenever I cross her path, she runs in the opposite direction. All I want to do is rub myself against her legs. Every time I try to show that woman affection, she just sneezes and acts like she'll die if we're in the same room.

I don't completely blame your mom. You never see positive portrayals of black cats on TV. Orange cats are used to sell cat food. And when an orange cat steals lasagna, it's sweet and funny. Orange cats are cute little guys who wear boots. But black cats? We're always demons and witches! That's some racist BS.

Love,
Coco

Dear Real Estate Agent,

My previous residence was a laundry basket. But it was lost in Hurricane Cleaning Lady. This box is cozy, though. Is this front window custom? I always wanted a nice view of people I could scratch if they got too close. And you say the previous owner was a microwave oven? I hope it didn't have any pets.

My housing needs are very particular. You see, I have a condition in which I'm deathly afraid of not being in small, confined places. I just can't handle the fear that when I'm not tucked into a tight space, the rocking chair might bite my tail again, or the little human who wears a litter box around his butt will chase me.

This place is perfect. I'll take it! Just tell me where to put my John Hancat. You can even close the lid right now if you want—I don't mind being a shut-in.

Love,
Moka

Name: Moka
Age: 11 Years
Re: Claw-strophobia

Name: Kitten
Age: 10 Months
Re: I never wanted you to see me like this

Dear Baby-Honey-Sweetheart,

Look, love of my nine lives. Hold on. It's not what it seems. I was just gonna pet it. That's why my paw is out. Don't look shocked. I'm not some violent predatory animal. My instinctual desire to smash this bug into goop was the old me. It was the kitten I was before I met you. You changed me. I'm still the same lovable guy you squeeze too tightly when you read romance novels. Do you remember our first date? You held me and I purred, and I licked your toes after you "accidentally" stepped in marinara sauce. That's who I am, babe. Kill this bug? No way. If you really want to know, he was a present for you. I was going to bring him to your front door and ask if we could adopt what was left of him.

You know I love you, baby,
Kitten

Dear Attention Giver,

I'm a very concerned little kitty. I've jumped onto your computer five times in the past twenty minutes, graciously offering to let you scratch my head. Yet every time, you push me off. What could possibly be more interesting than petting me until I inexplicably tire of you, swat your hand, and then run away? What were you about to do? Go onto a social network, maybe a chat room? Don't you know that people get adorable kitties like me so they don't have to have social lives? How can our relationship blossom if you try to develop normal human relationships?

And who is that whisker-faced trollop on your screen? What does she have that I don't? Why don't you stop fantasizing about some cat who doesn't even know you exist, and give me a head scratch. Pleeeease. You feed me, so I care about you a lot. I know that some cats are aloof. But I'm not one to play hard to pet.

Love,
Snow

Name: Snow
Age: 5 Weeks
Re: Chat room? I think you meant "cat room"

Name: Tussi
Age: 6 Years
Re: You didn't tell me you have humans . . . I'm allergic to humans

Dear Nasal Irritant,

As you know, I'm not just a kitty cat. I am an alien from a distant planet sent to Earth to study the effects of sleeping on heating vents. But my work has been disrupted by a series of uncontrollable cat sneezes. And you know what, human? Laughing at me is not helping. You probably think that with all the hair kitties shed, and all the allergy attacks we cause, it serves us right to occasionally have adorable little sneezing fits. But did you know that cat sneezes can actually be the sign of a bacterial infection? That would make sense, since I live with you, and I have never once seen you lick yourself clean. Or the sneezes might be from accidentally getting litter dust up my nose. But I haven't done that since I was a roadie for Faster Pussycat. Plus, I typically poop in the neighbor's vegetable garden.

No, the reason I am sneezing is because you're wearing too much of that new Kim Kardashian perfume. If you wanted to smell like a feral cat, you should've just asked. I would've been more than happy to spray you myself.

Love,
Tussi

Dear Enabler,

Maybe I do have anger issues. I admit, I can't stop after shredding one square. I go until the roll's completely ripped. If you tried to separate me from the toilet paper, I'd scratch you. I'm hurting the ones I love.

I've been a shred-head for as long as I can remember—and my mommy was also known to be found on the bathroom floor, covered in two-ply. Do you think I should enter a twelve-step program? I'd probably just sit under the steps and swat at people as they walked up.

But you keep putting out fresh rolls, enabling my problem. Please keep the toilet paper in a drawer and out of my sight. Once I see the white stuff I go crazy.

However, maybe I should hide the toilet paper from *you*. What I do to it isn't nearly as bad as what you do.

One day at a time,
Squishie

Name: Squishie
Age: 4 Years
Re: Signs that a kitty might have an anger management problem

Name: Sugar
Age: 3 Years
Re: Why can't you love me for who I am?

Dear Master,

I should've known this day would come. Last night when you were petting me, you said, "Who's a good kitty?" That's how you talk to a dog! Cats don't care if they're good. You clearly want someone who is in constant need of approval. Why don't you just get a dumb doggie, if you want one so much. I'm sure you can find some idiot pooch who will balance food on his nose, or go crazy when you say the word *jogging*. I'm sorry you can't go jogging with a kitty. But have you ever thought that with me you don't need to jog—I'm happy ignoring you just the way you are.

Love,
Sugar

Dear Bartender,

I heard the water running and decided to drop in to the sink for happy hour. Yes, I will have a drink, thank you. Whatever you have on tap is fine. When I was a young kitten and didn't know any better, I would drink from my water bowl. It's all I could get my paws on (which made quite a mess). But it's so stale tasting compared to a sip right from the source. Plus, once in a while when I go to the water dish, there's another cat in the bowl who stares at me. And he's very protective of his water, because the closer I get, the closer he gets. He's fast, too, because when I swat at him he immediately disappears.

But I like what you did with this place. I think this used to be a bathtub, right? That place sucked. I'm glad they pulled the plug on that joint.

Oh what, closing time already? That's fine. I know the bathroom faucet will open for after-dinner drinks.

Love,
Biscuit

Name: Biscuit
Age: 1 Year
Re: Bartender, what do you have on tap?

Name: Tasha
Age: 1 Year
Re: I'm glad my short-term memory problems amuse you

Dear Cat Startler,

What is it? Do I have something on my face? Why are you laughing? I was going to do something, but now I can't remember what it was. Don't you hate that? Since I am a cat, and I'm not asleep, I was probably licking myself and forgot to put my tongue back in my face. Is that why you're laughing at me? You know, if you spent a third of your life grooming, you, too, would occasionally forget to pull your tongue back in. And imagine the look on your face if someone walked in on you licking yourself. Your tongue would be the last thing you'd think about putting away. And you would certainly hope they didn't have a camera.

    Now, if you'll excuse me, I still have to wash behind my tail— and I don't think you want a picture of that.

Love,
Tasha

Dear Subjects to the Throne of Calvin,

It is an honor to be your king. And let me say that I was not born as your furry highness, eye level to the toilet paper roll, surveyor of all sinks that drip. I was once a common box user. I know what it's like to toil and bury, to go to sleep with clay under my claws. But no more am I banished to a stinky corner of the garage! I have risen up, and in so doing released my subjects from the feudal tyranny of scooping clumps. To celebrate, we will have games. Subjects, fetch me your finest string!

Love,
King Calvin the 1st and 2nd

Name: Calvin
Age: 2 Years
Re: I am King Calvin, but you may call me Lord John

Name: Marko
Age: 2 Months
Re: Let this be a warning to your toes

Dear Bringer of Pests,

You see this dead mousy? This is what happens when you cross Marko's floor without saying, "Hi, Marko kitty," and scratching my head. I know you might be tempted to remove the body, but don't! Another mousy looking and smelling exactly like him will just show up tomorrow, and I'll have to kill him all over again. I don't know how the exact same mousy keeps reappearing, but I'm a busy kitty, and I have socks to chew through and tinfoil balls to knock under the couch. I can't spend every day killing a mousy I could swear I already killed. So please, leave it out to remind the mouse that he is actually dead, and I'm bored with him.

Love,
Marko the Magnificent

Huge thanks to the extremely talented photographers who blessed this book with their work:

Carter Belleau, Moka, page 45; Elizabeth Blake, Isaac, page 29; Catherine Chanel, Coco, page 42; CitiKitty Pet Products, Calvin, page 61; David Clemmons (spacemouses), Kitten, page 46; Betsy Cole, Muffin, page 21, and Cherry, page 34; Dave DeHetre, Marko, page 62; Joan De Lurio, Didjeradoo, page 38; Sandy Ellis, Bubba, page 19; Fearon-Wood Photography, Fuzzy Wuzzy, page 41; Carolyn Ganus, Biscuit, page 57; Linda M. Goodman, Daisy, page 33; William H. Haas, Jillian, page 26; Staffan Hamnas, Tussi, page 51; Jason Hitchens, Maggie, page 30; Andrey Hristov, Charlie, page 25; Marjorie Lear, Macho, page 37; Loriann Morris, Squishie, page 53; Leta Paine, Tippy, page 10; Jodi Payne, Tasha, page 58; Edward H. Pien, Mia, page 22; Niklas Pivic, Blixa, Tiramisu, and Zabaglione, page 18, and Hendrix, page 8; Paula Rivas, Loli and the Teddy Bears, page 15; Peder Sandholm, Ili, page 14; Jaret Segovia, Dakota, page 11; Jixue Yang, Snow, page 49; Jia Zhang, Sugar, page 54.